WHERE IS ALLAH?

CHILDREN'S FIRST QUESTIONS

Written & Illustrated by Emma Apple

For The Baby

Copyright © 2016 Emma Apple

All rights reserved. This book or any portion thereof may not be reproduced or used in any manner without the express written permission of the copyright holder.

Books by Emma Apple – Chicago IL USA

First Edition - 2017 Update.

ISBN-13: 978-0692648278

www.emmaapple.com

BISMILLAH AR-RAHMAN AR-RAHEEM
WITH GOD'S NAME

The aim of this book is to explain that Allah has no measurable place in creation, though He knows what's in our hearts wherever we are.

We hope that this will help our children to know their creator and to look closer at the natural world to understand Him.

WHERE IS ALLAH?

Have you ever wondered where Allah is?

Can we find His place?

Allah says in the Qur'an, that He rose over His throne, above Jannah.

Does that mean Allah is up above us?

Which way is up anyway?

The Earth is a rotating sphere, so no direction can truly be up when we are on it and it is moving all the time. Up simply means, away from the Earth, towards the sky and into space.

On Earth we use North, South, East and West, to measure where things are compared to ourselves.

But in space, direction can't be measured this way, so we use the position of the stars and planets. There is no up, no north, south, east or west, but it is still within Allah's creation.

What if all the stars and planets disappeared?

Would we know where we are?

Without the stars and planets to guide us, we would not know our place, we find our way using Allah's creation.

Allah created a sense of direction for us, so that we know where we are and where we are going.

He is not restricted by direction and we cannot measure His place. He is above and outside creation, in every direction, wherever we turn.

Look for the signs of Allah all around you, read the Qur'an and pray to Him. This is the only way to truly understand His Greatness, His Beauty and that He is near us, even while He is outside creation.

Allah does not have a place the same way we do, but He knows everything in our hearts, wherever we are.

QUR'AN
SURAH 7 AL-A'RAF, AYAH 54

"Your Lord is Allah, The One Who created the heavens and the earth in six days, and then He rose over the Throne. He covers the night with the day, each seeking the other in rapid succession. And the sun, the moon, and the stars, are under His command. Surely for Him is the creation and the command. Blessed is Allah, the Lord of the worlds!"

How GPS Works

When you need directions while driving, you use a GPS, a device with a map that can calculate where you are and guide you to where you need to go.

GPS stands for Global Positioning System and it's a network of about 30 satellites that orbit the Earth about 12,000 miles above us. They send signals down to your GPS device and figure out your location based on how long it takes for the signal to get back to the satellite. This process is called *trilateration*. Wherever you are on Earth, at least 4 satellites are above you, the more satellites that can "see" you, the more accurate your location will be on your GPS device.

How Do They Navigate In Space?

The people managing the space probes and their missions (like NASA) start by planning where they're going and how they'll get there. They use accurate maps of the solar system and calculations of where planets and other objects in the solar system will be, to make these plans.

Once the probe has left Earth, the people managing the mission use the Deep Space Network (DSN), a series of 3 radio antennae on Earth that send and receive radio signals and measure how long they take to return (like a GPS, but for the solar system). This measures the speed and location of a space probe. The probes have all of the instructions they need before they even leave Earth, but humans on the ground are able to use the DSN to send commands and corrections if they need to. They can also receive information about what the probe finds out there, using the same Deep Space Network.

How A Compass Works

Earth has an inner core at its center made of solid metal and an outer core around that made of hot liquid metal, both are made of a mix of Iron (Fe) and Nickel (Ni). The outer core is always moving, this movement generates a magnetic field around the planet, making Earth into a giant magnet! Like every magnet, Earth has a north pole and a south pole which other magnets respond to.

Most magnets we use don't respond to the magnetic field because they can't move freely, but a compass is made with a very light magnet that is able to spin freely, so it responds to Earths magnetic field, and points to the north pole.

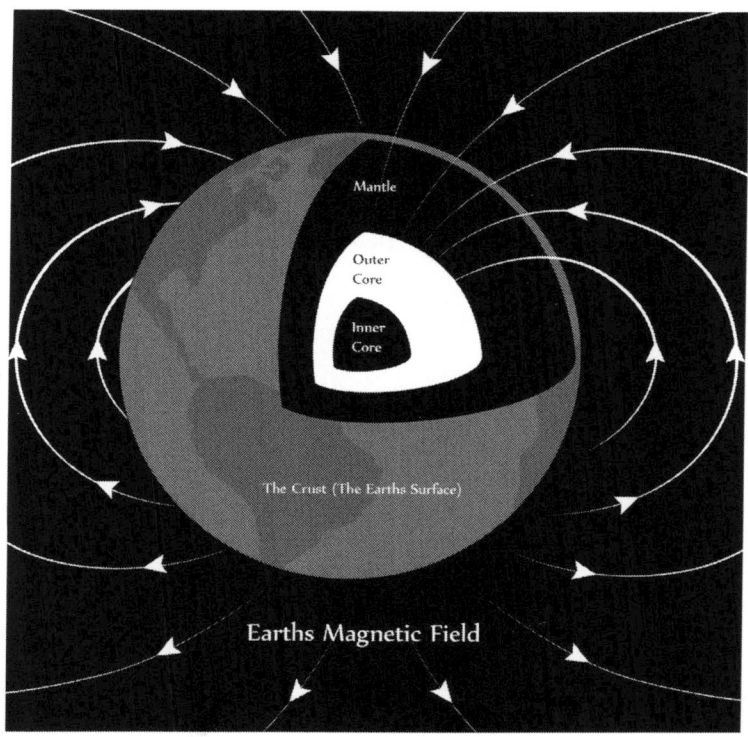

GLOSSARY

Throne - A chair for a ruler.

Jannah - Heaven.

Sphere - A 3 dimensional round shape, like a ball.

Rotating - Turning around in circles.

Measure - To calculate the size or amount of something.

Compare - To measure how similar or different things are.

Direction - The path where something moves, lies or points.

Position - The place where something is located.

Guide - To show someone the way.

Restricted - Limited in some way.

BOOKS BY EMMA APPLE

The Best Selling Children's First Questions Series:
Book 1: How Big Is Allah?
Book 2: How Does Allah Look?
Book 3: Where Is Allah?
Book 4: Is Allah Real?

The Owl and Cat Series:
Owl & Cat: Ramadan Is...
Owl & Cat: Islam Is...
Owl & Cat: Family Is...

Find more from Emma Apple online at www.emmaapple.com

Printed in Great Britain
by Amazon